HAPPY
HOUSEPLANTS

HAPPY HOUSEPLANTS

30 LOVELY VARIETIES TO BRIGHTEN UP YOUR HOME

~ ANGELA STAEHLING ~

CHRONICLE BOOKS

SAN FRANCISCO

Library of Congress Cataloging-in-Publication Data available.

ISBN 978-1-4521-6146-4

Manufactured in China

Designed by Allison Weiner
Typesetting by Howie Severson

10 9 8 7 6 5 4 3 2

Chronicle books and gifts are available at special quantity discounts to corporations, professional associations, literacy programs, and other organizations. For details and discount information, please contact our premiums department at corporatesales@chroniclebooks.com or at 1-800-759-0190.

Chronicle Books LLC
680 Second Street
San Francisco, California 94107
www.chroniclebooks.com

To my kids, Cole, Mia, and Ella,
in the hopes that they embrace the joys of gardening someday.

Contents

Introduction

IMAGINE YOURSELF in a tranquil setting, birds chirping, the scent of wild-flowers all around while you breathe in the fresh air. Sounds good, right? Nature has the power to relax, restore, and rejuvenate. So why not bring a hint of that blissful goodness right into your home?

Houseplants can spruce up any indoor space. But for some of us, growing these green lovelies and tending to their needs is intimidating. Caring for the life of any organism can be daunting at first. Luckily, sustaining happy houseplants is actually pretty simple and, in the end, is a rewarding experience.

This book lays out the basic rules of thumb for growing thirty popular and easy-to-grow plants inside the home. Most plants have four basic needs: sunlight, water, soil, and fertilizer. In the following pages, I've outlined variations on these needs in each plant's Step-by-Step Care section. Follow the right recipe for your plants' needs and you can expect to have some happy houseplants at your side.

Most greenhouse experts will tell you that the more they learn about plants, the more they realize is yet to be learned—so keep an open mind and go easy on yourself. Slight fluctuations in temperature, humidity, and sunlight often occur throughout your home without your realizing it, and these changes, however small, can impact the life and health of your houseplants. The more you grow houseplants, the more familiar you'll become with the nuanced needs of each type of plant and the differences in conditions around your space.

Make no mistake: there are fussy plants that will test your wits. If a temperamental plant is looking sickly after you've given it everything you think it needs, don't give up. You can simply try switching things around to find the plant's perfect growing conditions. Sometimes little things have the biggest impact on the health of your plant—a nudge closer to the window, less water to prevent root rot, or a nutritious boost of fertilizer. And if your love of one plant has completely faded, feel free to move on; there are plenty of others that would adore being in your home.

After neglecting some of my plants and smothering others with too much attention, I have learned over the years that finding a happy medium is key. Houseplants simply need a little love and care—not too much—and they will happily thrive for years to come.

Happy planting!

Getting Started

GROWING AND CARING FOR the thirty plants in this book only requires a few common tools and materials (some of which you may already have stashed around the house). Stock up on these basics and you can start creating a home full of happy houseplants in no time.

Tools

GLOVES

As adorable as they look hanging in the checkout lanes at your local nursery, gardening gloves often get overlooked when it comes to indoor planting. But trust me, as soon as you start getting your hands dirty, you'll be wishing for a pair. They do much more than prevent black soil from getting wedged under your fingernails—gloves prevent your skin from drying out and protect hands from spines and sharp leaves. (They are mandatory when it comes to handling cacti.)

Gardening gloves come in various sizes and different materials such as cloth, rubber, leather, suede, or synthetic blends. Thicker, heavier fabrics work for holding cacti, whereas thinner, less bulky gloves are better for handling delicate plants. For most indoor planting, a lightweight cloth or nylon glove with a nitrile (rubber alternative) palm is all you need.

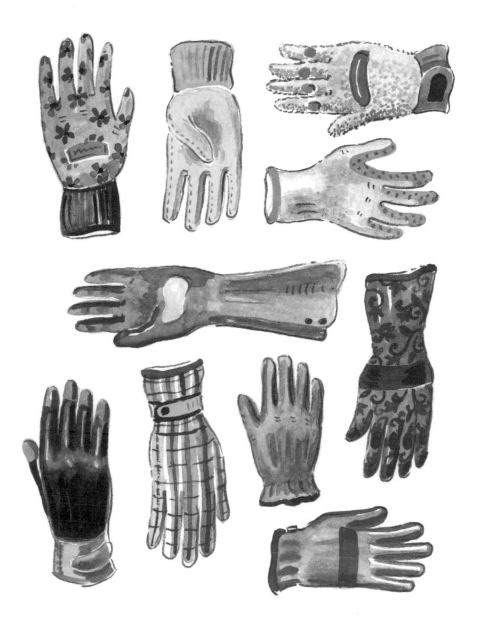

HAND TOOLS

There are three basic hand tools used in indoor gardening: cultivators, transplanters, and trowels. You don't need to own all three, but I recommend purchasing any tool that makes your experience of indoor gardening more pleasurable. These tools are widely available and luckily not too expensive. Some companies even sell them as a set of three.

CULTIVATOR: A cultivator is a hand rake that can be used to aerate compacted soil, mix granular fertilizer into soil before watering, and loosen roots when repotting.

TRANSPLANTER: A transplanter is a narrow trowel with depth measurements on the spade for quick reference, designed for easy transplanting of plants.

TROWEL: This small tool with a curved scoop is used for breaking up soil, digging holes, lifting plants, and planting bulbs.

PRUNING TOOLS

There are several different tools you can use to trim unwanted material from your plants. While a sturdy pair of scissors or sharp knife could do the trick, cutters specifically designed for plants usually yield better results (plus you don't dull your knives or scissors in the process).

PRUNING SHEARS: Also called hand pruners, pruning shears make clean cuts that heal quickly. They are ideal for trimming woody stems and snipping off roots when cutting back a root ball (a mass formed by roots and soil). There are two basic types of pruners: bypass and anvil. Bypass pruners (the most popular type) have two curved blades that move past each other like a pair of scissors. These pruners work well for live stems and roots. Anvil pruners use one sharp blade to cut against a flat edge, much like a knife on a chopping board. Anvil pruners are heavy duty and work well on tough, dry, and dead stems.

GARDEN SCISSORS: This variety of scissors is typically more delicate than pruning shears, making them perfect for deadheading (snipping off spent flower blooms) and making precision cuts. Some garden scissors have large handle hoops to accommodate your whole hand for a more secure grip.

GARDEN SNIPS: Like garden scissors, garden snips work well for light pruning and trimming. Snips are spring-loaded to reduce hand stress when making numerous cuts. These cutters are ideal for shaping small plants.

WATERING CONTAINERS

All plants need some form of water. Although watering cans will do the trick for most common houseplants, there are special options for humidity-loving plants. No matter the type, these watering vessels can look adorable displayed on a shelf or next to your favorite plant.

MISTERS: Misters, or spray bottles, emit a soft spray of water and work well on humidity-loving plants such as mosses, ferns, and air plants. While many houseplants enjoy a light misting (even to clean dust off of the leaves), regularly watering the soil is most beneficial because plants absorb essential nutrients from their roots. Succulents or desert plants prefer drier air and do not need to be misted.

WATERING CANS: Watering cans, the most common type of watering container, come in a variety of shapes, sizes, and materials. Some watering cans come with a detachable sprinkle head, also known as a "rose," which allows for a diffused spray that is easier on tender stems and blooms. Tilt your rose slightly upward for an even softer fountain. Pick a watering can you love, because you will use it all the time!

WATERING TIP: If you are concerned about too much chlorine in your water, allow your full watering container to sit out for twelve to twenty-four hours, uncovered, to let the chlorine evaporate before sharing the water with your plants. Too much chlorine can be a problem for some plants.

Materials

FERTILIZER

Fertilizer, or all-purpose plant food, adds beneficial nutrients to soil. Plants especially crave extra nutrients to feed themselves through high-growth periods, namely spring through autumn. Feed plants when you water to allow nutrients to evenly disperse throughout the soil. Since newly purchased plants or plants that have been repotted in fresh potting mix will typically have fertilizer already in the soil, wait at least six weeks for the existing fertilizer to dissipate before adding your own, because too much fertilizer can be detrimental to a plant. I've specified the types and amounts of fertilizer to use for each of the thirty plants in this book.

There are three basic components of fertilizer: nitrogen, phosphorous, and potassium. You will find these nutrients represented as numbers on the label of your houseplant fertilizer, for example 10-30-20. The first number is nitrogen, which helps leaves and new stems grow. The second number represents phosphorous, a nutrient responsible for producing healthy flowers and roots. The third number is potassium, which is needed for overall plant health. Balanced houseplant fertilizers have numbers that are close in range, such as 6-5-6. The most common types of fertilizer come in liquid or powder crystals.

POTS AND CONTAINERS

Pots and containers can turn an already beautiful plant into home décor. With so many adorable flowerpot options, you might have a hard time deciding whether to buy new or to use an antique or family heirloom. Either way, there are a few things to keep in mind when selecting containers for your houseplants.

MATERIAL: Some flowerpots are porous, such as terra-cotta and clay, and will absorb excess water from the soil. This helps prevent your roots from getting too soggy and rotting. Terra-cotta and clay pots are the best choices for many houseplants. Cacti, succulents, and bromeliads especially love terra-cotta and clay because their soil needs to thoroughly dry between waterings. You'll need to water your houseplants more frequently in terra-cotta and clay pots.

Containers made of plastic, glass, metal, fiberglass, and ceramic are great choices for houseplants too. These containers are not porous and will hold water for longer durations.

However, you will have to be mindful to not overwater. Most roots don't do well in wet soil for extended periods.

DRAINAGE: Regardless of the type of pot you choose, be sure it has adequate drainage at the bottom. A saucer or plastic liner placed underneath your pot will hold any excess water that drains away from the soil. Make sure to empty the saucer if it fills up with water. Roots don't like sitting in soggy soil. Some pots may not have drainage holes but are shallow and wide enough to allow for water to evaporate from the soil.

If you have a narrow or tall container that does not have drainage holes, you can either drill holes in the bottom (depending upon the material of the pot) or place one container (with drainage holes) inside of your chosen container. This outer container is called a cache pot. I recommend setting a saucer underneath your inner pot. Another option is to place pebbles in the bottom of the outer pot to allow the water to drain away from the roots in the inner pot.

SIZE: Size is also important. Select a container that will hold enough potting mix for your roots to spread out. You don't want to squeeze a plant into a container that is too small, as this will crowd the roots and impede the plant's growth.

Plants become root-bound when they outgrow their pots. Signs of this condition include roots extending above the soil or poking through drainage holes. Typically, plants will not create any new growth or will produce only small leaves when this happens. To save your plant, you can (1) repot your plant in a larger container, (2) remove your plant from the container, trim back some roots, and replant into the same container, or (3) divide your plant in half—if it has multiple stems at the soil's surface—and create two potted plants.

REPOTTING: Houseplants benefit from being repotted every two to three years. Nutrients in the soil get used up by the roots and also are washed out after many waterings. Plants perform best when repotted in spring, as new growth appears.

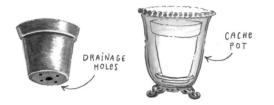

DRAINAGE HOLES

CACHE POT

QUICK GUIDE TO REPOTTING

1. Water your plant to soften the soil.

2. Turn the old container on its side. Support the main stem with your hand while tapping the outside of the pot to loosen the soil. Using a transplanter or trowel, break the soil away from the inside edge of the pot. Carefully remove the plant from the pot with your hands.

3. Try to loosen any roots with your fingers or a trowel. Using pruners or a sharp knife, trim loosened roots to the depth of the container you wish to use. If the roots are wound too tightly and cannot be loosened, cut off the bottom layer of the root ball (up to one-third). Slice 1 inch / 2.5 cm slabs off the vertical edges around the root ball. Your plant will appreciate the trim. If your soil is not root-bound, gently shake off and discard any soil between the roots that looks powdery or mildewy. Otherwise, try to leave the soil intact. Carefully snip off any dead or rotten roots.

4. If you're repotting the plant in the same container, sterilize the container by soaking it in a bleach solution of nine parts water to one part household bleach for at least ten minutes. Wipe dry before replanting.

5. Pour fresh potting mix into the container to create a small mound at the bottom. Place the plant in the container so the root crown (area of the root system where stems arise) rests about ½ inch / 12 mm below the rim of the pot. Add potting mix around the edges, pressing down with your fingers to remove air pockets.

6. Water the plant thoroughly until water seeps from the drainage holes. Add extra potting mix if the soil settles below ½ inch / 12 mm from the rim. (You may want to water in a sink or outside so you can wash away soil that has dirtied up the container during the transplant.)

7. Wait at least one month and then fertilize. Your plant needs to recover from the stress of repotting first. Most potting mixes already include fertilizer, so adding more isn't necessary.

POTTING MIXES

Let's dish the dirt—not all potting mixtures are created equal. While an all-purpose potting mix is the most popular choice for indoor plants, some plants, like the cactus and African violet, prefer their own special blends of ingredients. As you read about the plants in this book, you'll learn the type of soil that is best suited for each plant.

ALL-PURPOSE POTTING MIX:

An all-purpose potting mix is typically a mixture of aged bark, peat moss, perlite (volcanic glass), lime (dolomite limestone), and compost. Other ingredients can include coir (coconut husk fiber), sand, vermicompost (worm castings), vermiculite (mineral deposit), bone meal, kelp meal, and gypsum. These ingredients provide nutrients and balance the pH levels (a measure of acidity or alkalinity) of your soil. Perlite and vermiculite also help conserve water while aerating your soil. You can buy an all-purpose potting mix at most garden centers, or you can create your own.

MAKE YOUR OWN ALL-PURPOSE POTTING MIX

One-third peat moss or coconut coir

One-third topsoil

One-third perlite or coarse sand (builder's sand)

1 teaspoon of lime mineral per gallon of soil (to help neutralize the pH level)

Thoroughly mix all ingredients and store in a covered container. Lightly moisten potting mix when ready to use.

ALL-PURPOSE POTTING MIX

PERLITE

VERMICULITE   PEAT MOSS   COCONUT COIR

LIME   COARSE SAND   VERMICOMPOST

BONE MEAL   KELP MEAL   GYPSUM

AFRICAN VIOLET POTTING MIX:
African violets require a special
potting mix that contains little or no
soil. The mix is light and airy to prevent the roots from getting weighed
down or compacted. Potting mix for
African violets is typically comprised
of peat moss, perlite, or other water-
conserving agents. You can buy pre-
mixed African violet potting mix or you
can create your own.

MAKE YOUR OWN AFRICAN VIOLET POTTING MIX

One-third peat moss
One-third vermiculite
One-third perlite

Thoroughly mix all ingredients and
store in a covered container. Lightly
moisten potting mix when ready
to use.

**CACTUS AND SUCCULENT
POTTING MIX:** Cactus and succulent
potting mix is formulated to drain water
out of soil more rapidly than other
potting soils, since these plants prefer
drier soil. You can purchase potting
mix already prepared for these fleshy
plants or, as some cactus and succulent
enthusiasts prefer to do, create your
own. Here is a basic recipe for mixing
up your own quick-drying potting mix.

MAKE YOUR OWN CACTUS AND SUCCULENT POTTING MIX

One-third all-purpose potting mix
One-third coarse sand
One-third perlite

Thoroughly mix all ingredients and
store in a covered container. Lightly
moisten potting mix when ready
to use.

The Happy Houseplants

African Violet

• *Saintpaulia ionantha* •

African violets have long been a popular plant sold seasonally for Valentine's Day, Easter, and Mother's Day. These tropical plants display colorful flowers in varying shades of purple, pink, white, blue, and red. For maximum flowering, keep African violets in ten to fourteen hours of bright, indirect light each day. Pinch off blooms as they fade to encourage the development of more flowers. The African violet prefers temperatures between 65° and 75°F / 18° and 24°C.

STEP-BY-STEP CARE

SOIL: Use an African violet potting mix, or make your own mixture of one-third peat moss, one-third vermiculite, and one-third perlite.

LIGHT: African violets prefer bright, indirect light. Place in an east-facing window to receive morning sun.

WATER: Keep soil evenly moist but not soggy. African violets are picky about their water.

When the soil feels dry to the touch, use room-temperature water to hydrate the plant. Avoid getting leaves wet, as this can lead to leaf spotting.

FERTILIZER: Fertilize every two weeks during summer with a high-phosphorous fertilizer, such as 15-30-15 (phosphorous is the middle number). This nutrient helps roots grow and stimulates flowering. A balanced houseplant fertilizer will also work.

TIP: African violets perform better when repotted every year. Remove one-third of the old soil and place the plant in a container that is slightly larger than the previous pot. Add African violet potting mix, making sure crown of the plant rests just below the soil line. Water thoroughly.

• Tillandsia •

An air plant is a tropical plant that comes in hundreds of varieties and is accustomed to growing on trees, rocks, other plants, and rocky cliffs. The bromeliads are a joy to grow, as they require no soil and look great hanging in unusual containers, architectural forms, and glass vases. Air plants can be mounted to other surfaces using adhesives like E6000, Liquid Nails, or hot glue. Make sure these surfaces are waterproof, as you will still need to water your plant. Fishing line, natural twine, or non-copper wire also work well to mount your plant.

STEP-BY-STEP CARE

SOIL: Air plants don't require soil to grow.

LIGHT: Air plants prefer bright, indirect light. They can tolerate a few hours of full sun but then will require more water.

WATER: Mist air plants once or twice a week depending on the humidity in your home. Give them an extra soak in a bowl of water for twenty to thirty minutes once a week. Gently shake off excess water.

FERTILIZER: Fertilizing air plants isn't necessary, but it can stimulate blooming and reproduction. Use a water-soluble bromeliad fertilizer (17-8-22) diluted to one-quarter strength. Add drops once a month during spring and summer when soaking plants in a bowl of water.

TIP: Trim off outer leaves if they become dry and lose color. This is normal as the plant grows or becomes acclimated to a new environment.

• Aloe vera •

The aloe vera plant is well known for its clear, cool gel that helps heal burns and cuts. Its thick, fleshy leaves point out in all directions and will have serrated edges or white spots, depending on the variety. When an aloe plant reaches maturity (at approximately four years of age), and if it receives enough light, it may produce a tall flowering stalk in spring. If you purchase your aloe plant in a small plastic container, consider repotting it in a larger clay container. Aloe plants become very top-heavy as they grow and will have a tendency to fall over. A heavy clay or terracotta pot will keep your plant stable.

STEP-BY-STEP CARE

SOIL: Use a cactus and succulent potting mix, or create your own quick-draining soil with one-third potting mix, one-third coarse sand, and one-third perlite. Add coconut coir or peat moss to help with water absorption and aeration.

LIGHT: Aloe vera plants prefer partial to direct sun in a west- or south-facing window. Rotate the pot once a week to promote upright growth. If leaves turn brown, provide less direct sun.

WATER: Water thoroughly and let the soil dry out between waterings. Water less in the winter. Aloe vera is a drought-tolerant plant and prefers drier soils.

FERTILIZER: Feed once a month during spring and summer with a houseplant fertilizer high in phosphorous, such as 10-40-10. Dilute fertilizer to half strength.

TIP: Trim your aloe plant if it has gotten too large. Cut off outer leaves first, as these are the older growth; new leaves emerge from the center of the plant. Remove any leaves that have turned brown or dried up.

AMARYLLIS

• Hippeastrum •

The amaryllis is the most popular flowering bulb to force indoors during the winter. Its large, flowering head sits atop a tall, stately stem and blooms in a variety of colors. Evergreen leaves jut out from the base of the plant to add striking contrast. Plant bulbs in November for a flowering display during the holidays. Use a heavy pot, as amaryllis can get top-heavy and topple in a lightweight plastic container. To plant a bulb, partially fill a container with soil and add the bulb. Fill in with more soil, keeping the bulb's neck above soil level. The warmer the temperature, the faster your bulb will grow.

STEP-BY-STEP CARE

SOIL: Use well-draining all-purpose potting mix.

LIGHT: The amaryllis prefers partial to full sun.

WATER: Water sparingly until growth appears, then water regularly. Keep soil moist but not soggy.

FERTILIZER: When flowers fade, remove blooms and cut back stems to 2 inches / 5 cm above the bulb. Continue to water and add a balanced houseplant fertilizer monthly during spring and summer. Stop watering in the fall and let bulbs rest for six weeks in a cool location (40° to 50°F / 4° to 10°C). Begin the growing process once again about 5 to 8 weeks before you want blooms.

TIP: Grow amaryllis in a glass vase with pebbles and water. Place 3 inches / 7.5 cm of pebbles in a vase. Set the amaryllis bulb on top, pointy side up, and add extra pebbles to secure the bulb. Pour in water to just below the base of the bulb. Regularly add water to keep it at the same level.

BLUE CHALK STICKS

• *Senecio mandraliscae* •

Blue chalk sticks are a popular, easy-to-grow indoor plant that adds stunning contrast against other foliage in a mixed container. The silvery blue pencil-like leaves curve upward along moderately growing stems. The plant will become leggy in form and can grow to a height of around 18 inches / 46 cm and spread to 24 inches / 61 cm wide. Pinch off any new growth, especially on the lower stems, to encourage a fuller plant. In summer, blue chalk sticks may grow small white flowers, which can be trimmed off to create a cleaner look.

STEP-BY-STEP CARE

SOIL: Use a cactus and succulent potting mix, or create your own quick-draining soil with one-third potting mix, one-third coarse sand, and one-third perlite.

LIGHT: Blue chalk sticks prefer partial to full sun.

WATER: Water thoroughly and let the soil dry out between waterings. Water less in the winter. Blue chalk sticks are drought tolerant and prefer drier soil.

FERTILIZER: Feed with a balanced houseplant fertilizer once a month during spring and summer. Dilute fertilizer to half strength.

TIP: Blue chalk sticks are easy to propagate. In spring, trim 2 to 3 inches / 5 to 7.5 cm off a stem, or more if the stem has gotten too leggy, and repot the trimming in a new container with cactus and succulent potting mix. Keep the soil moist but not soggy. New roots will begin to grow in about one week.

• *Sedum morganianum* •

The burro's tail cactus has long draping stems with thick overlapping leaves, resembling a braided donkey's tail. The blue-green succulent, also known as the donkey tail plant, looks striking in a hanging basket near a window. Keep temperatures between 65° and 75°F / 18° and 24°C, and keep the plant away from cool drafts. The burro tail's stems can grow 3 feet / 91 cm long and they require little maintenance.

STEP-BY-STEP CARE

SOIL: Use a cactus and succulent potting mix, or create your own quick-draining soil with one-third potting mix, one-third coarse sand, and one-third perlite. Add vermicompost to provide extra nutrients and beneficial enzymes.

LIGHT: Place burro's tail cactus in bright light. Morning sun is fine. Hot afternoon sun can burn the leaves and turn them pale green.

WATER: Water thoroughly and let the soil dry out between waterings. The burro's tail cactus is drought tolerant and prefers drier soils.

FERTILIZER: Feed with a balanced houseplant fertilizer once a month during spring and summer. Dilute fertilizer to half strength.

TIP: Plant your burro's tail cactus in a hanging pot with other succulents for a beautiful display of color and texture.

• Capsicum annuum •

Chili pepper plants are not only a treat to have at your culinary fingertips, they are also a decorative houseplant to brighten up your kitchen. Most indoor chili plants are dwarf varieties, so they grow smaller in scale than their outdoor counterparts. The ornamental plant comes in a variety of cultivars with the peppers growing in varying shades of red, orange, yellow, purple, black, and white. All fruits are edible but tend to be hot and spicy. Keep temperatures between 70° and 80°F / 21° and 26°C during the day and 55° and 65°F / 13° and 18°C at night.

STEP-BY-STEP CARE

SOIL: Use good-quality all-purpose potting mix, or make your own mixture of one-half peat moss with one-half perlite or vermiculite.

LIGHT: Place the chili plant in full sun for at least six hours a day. Lack of bright light will result in narrower stems and fewer peppers.

WATER: Thoroughly soak the soil until water drips from the drainage holes. If the saucer under the pot fills with water, empty it. Don't water again until the soil is slightly dry to the touch.

FERTILIZER: Feed with a balanced houseplant fertilizer twice a month during spring and summer. Stop feeding when the plant is finished producing fruit.

TIP: For a more bushy appearance, trim some stems back to encourage new growth. To harvest peppers, cut stems just above the fruit.

CUSHION MOSS

• *Leucobryum glaucum* •

A shade-loving plant, cushion moss thrives in a damp, humid environment much like the forest floor. Sometimes called pincushion moss or white cushion moss, this lush, velvety plant gives a perfect woodland touch to any potted plant or glass terrarium. To grow in a terrarium, first set a layer of rocks or pebbles in a glass container for proper drainage. Next, place a layer of horticultural charcoal (found at your local garden center) to help keep the air fresh and to retain moisture. Add soil to a depth of the first two layers combined and press down firmly. Place moss on top of the soil and add decorative elements, such as stones, branches, or figurines.

STEP-BY-STEP CARE

SOIL: Add peat moss to all-purpose potting mix to increase acidity. Soil needs to have a pH of 5.0 to 6.0. If the potting mix is fluffy, push it down firmly before placing the moss on top.

LIGHT: Most mosses prefer partial shade, however, a couple hours of morning sun will work for most types of moss.

WATER: If growing in a closed terrarium, mist the moss regularly during the first three weeks after planting to get it established. Leave the lid slightly open to aerate the container. Once established, mist less often. Keep the container damp but not soggy. If using an open container, mist daily to keep moist.

FERTILIZER: Mosses don't need fertilizer indoors.

TIP: Search for mosses in a local wooded area for your container garden. Use a butter knife, or any flat-bladed tool, to carefully remove it, leaving some soil intact on the underside. Check for insects or mold by rinsing the moss and removing any debris. Place moss in a partially sealed plastic zippered bag and set it in indirect sun. Spritz with water if the moss dries out. If no insects or mold appear after four days, your moss should be fine to use.

• Adenium obesum •

The desert rose is most notable for its flowered canopy atop a swollen woody stem. Native to Africa, the desert rose stores water in its trunk and is drought tolerant. It can be grown as a bonsai tree (an ornamental tree grown in a container). Keep temperatures above 65°F / 18°C, as this succulent thrives in a warm to hot climate. The desert rose may have a dormancy period in winter where it will lose some or all of its leaves. Provide enough sun and warmth in spring and the plant will fill out with new growth. Choose a clay or terra-cotta pot to help draw water away from the soil and prevent it from becoming soggy.

STEP-BY-STEP CARE

SOIL: Use a quick-draining soil mixture or cactus soil mix. Add peat moss to your soil to make it slightly acidic. The desert rose prefers a soil pH of 6.0.

LIGHT: Place the desert rose in full sun. The stem will lean as it grows toward the sun, especially if the plant is young, so rotate the pot every few days to keep the stem straight.

WATER: Thoroughly soak the plant until water drips from the drainage holes. If the saucer beneath the pot fills with water, empty it. Don't water again until the soil is slightly dry to the touch. Water less during winter.

FERTILIZER: Feed with a balanced houseplant fertilizer every two weeks during spring. When growth slows in early summer, switch fertilizers and feed once with a slow-release palm fertilizer, which will feed the plant extra nitrogen, helping to develop a deeper root system and keep foliage lush. Do this once again in fall.

TIP: Prune your desert rose in spring to promote the growth of more branches and fuller foliage. Cut back new growth thoughtfully, leaving some in place. Remove any new leaves and stems from the base of the plant.

• *Acanthocereus tetragonus 'Fairy Castles'* •

The fairy castle cactus is one of the most popular choices for indoor plants because of its easy maintenance. With emerald green spires that tower straight up like turrets on a castle, this sun-loving plant is a slow grower. Your newly purchased fairy castle cactus may come adorned with a colorful flower perched on its top. Chances are it's a straw flower glued on to accessorize your cactus. Feel free to remove the flower if you'd prefer your plant au naturel.

STEP-BY-STEP CARE

SOIL: Use a cactus and succulent potting mix, or create your own quick-draining soil with one-third potting mix, one-third coarse sand, and one-third perlite.

LIGHT: Place the fairy castle cactus in full sun. Rotate your plant periodically to prevent it from leaning too far in the direction of the sun.

WATER: Thoroughly soak the plant until water drips from the drainage holes. Let the soil dry out completely before the next watering. Water less during the winter.

FERTILIZER: Feed with a cactus fertilizer diluted to half strength every two weeks during spring and summer. Or use a low-nitrogen fertilizer, such as 5-10-10, once every two months during the growing season, diluted to half strength. The fairy castle cactus does not need fertilizer during fall and winter. If repotting, wait two months before fertilizing.

TIP: Consider using a terra-cotta pot or other porous container so that water in the soil can evaporate more quickly.

False Shamrock

• *Oxalis triangularis* •

The flowering false shamrock grows from a bulb and is often sold around St. Patrick's Day. This plant with three triangular leaves is also known as the purple shamrock or wood sorrel and displays small white or pale pink flowers during spring and summer. Like other bulb-based plants, the false shamrock can go into dormancy a couple of times a year, especially if indoor temperatures rise above 80°F / 27°C. The false shamrock prefers temperatures between 60° and 70°F / 16° and 21°C. When the foliage dies off, stop watering and feeding the plant. Remove the dead leaves and stems, and the bulbs will begin to grow again in about two to four weeks. At this time, resume watering and feeding your plant.

STEP-BY-STEP CARE

SOIL: Use good-quality all-purpose potting mix.

LIGHT: Place your false shamrock in bright light but not direct sun. Your plant can tolerate partial shade.

WATER: Water regularly, allowing the top 1 to 2 inches / 2.5 to 5 cm of soil to dry out between waterings. Do not water when the plant has gone dormant (that is, when the foliage withers and dies off).

FERTILIZER: Feed with a balanced houseplant fertilizer once a month. Do not feed during dormancy.

TIP: Don't be alarmed if your plant's leaves close up. The false shamrock has a photonastic response, which means the leaves open during the daytime and close at night. If your leaves stay closed, try giving them a little more sunlight.

• Euphorbia tirucalli •

The firestick cactus—also known as fire pencil, sticks on fire, or milkbush—sports vibrant shades of red, orange, and yellow at the tips of its stems. These fiery hues become more intense on new growth and when the plant receives lots of sunlight. The colors will fade and turn to green as the plant ages. Place your plant in a cool location during autumn and winter, and you should see a burst of color again. Remember to still give your firestick plenty of sunshine. Gloves and long sleeves are recommended when handling the firestick, as its milky white sap (a natural form of latex) can cause skin irritation, especially around the face and eyes.

STEP-BY-STEP CARE

SOIL: Use a cactus and succulent potting mix, or create your own quick-draining soil with one-third potting mix, one-third coarse sand, and one-third perlite.

LIGHT: Place your firestick cactus in a west- or south-facing window. This plant loves full sun.

WATER: Water thoroughly every two to three weeks in spring and summer, allowing soil to dry out between waterings. Water less during fall and winter.

FERTILIZER: Feed with a balanced houseplant fertilizer every two weeks, spring through fall. For best results, dilute fertilizer to half of the normal strength.

TIP: Consider using a terra-cotta pot or other porous container so that water in the soil can evaporate more quickly.

• Asparagus densiflorus 'Myers' •

The foxtail fern is, surprisingly, not a fern at all. A member of the lily family, the foxtail fern has tiny needlelike leaves on each frond, creating a bushy shape that resembles fluffy foxtails. Also known as the asparagus fern or Myers asparagus, this striking and architecturally interesting plant can grow up to 2 feet / 61 cm tall by 2 to 3 feet / 61 to 91 cm wide. In late spring to early summer, the foxtail fern will produce small white flowers that set to seed as red berries. Foxtail plumes make wonderful additions to floral arrangements.

STEP-BY-STEP CARE

SOIL: Use good-quality all-purpose potting mix. The addition of peat moss will ensure good drainage, as the soil should not be allowed to get soggy.

WATER: Water thoroughly, allowing the soil to dry out between waterings. Foxtail ferns enjoy higher humidity and benefit from occasional misting. Water less during the winter months.

LIGHT: Foxtail ferns grow well in moderate to bright light. The more indirect sun the plant receives, the quicker it will grow. The foxtail fern can tolerate full morning sun.

FERTILIZER: Feed with a balanced houseplant fertilizer once a month from spring through fall. For best results, dilute fertilizer to half strength.

TIP: If the foxtail fern's leaves turn yellow, provide more water. If the leaves turn brown, reduce the amount of water. Trim off any faded fronds to encourage new growth.

GRAPE HYACINTH

• *Muscari armeniacum* •

Naturally a spring-flowering bulb, grape hyacinths can be forced to bloom indoors to brighten up your winter. Plant bulbs in early autumn in a 6-inch / 15-cm tall container with good drainage holes and fill soil to within 2 inches / 5 cm of the rim. With pointy sides up, set the bulbs on top of the soil 1 to 2 inches / 2.5 to 5 cm apart. Place more soil over the bulbs until they are lightly covered. Gently water and place the pot in a cool, dark location (35° to 50°F / 2° to 10°C) for about ten weeks. When growth is at least 1 inch / 2.5 cm above the soil, set the container in a slightly warmer location (50° to 65°F / 10° to 18°C) with partial to full sunlight.

STEP-BY-STEP CARE

SOIL: Use good-quality all-purpose potting mix.

LIGHT: Keep the bulbs in a dark location until leaves emerge above the soil. Then, move the container to a bright, slightly cool space in your home to promote flowering.

WATER: Check bulbs weekly to see if the soil is dry. If so, gently water to keep the soil lightly moist.

FERTILIZER: Feed with a balanced houseplant fertilizer every ten days when growth appears. Stop fertilizing when flowers fade.

TIP: Grape hyacinths will bloom longer if kept in cool, indirect sunlight. For a longer show of blooms, plant several in multiple pots and then bring them out into bright, cool locations a week or two apart through winter. When flowers fade, plant the bulbs outside in your garden as perennials.

• Sempervivum tectorum •

Hen and chicks is a favorite of many gardeners. This succulent comes in a variety of colors, shapes, and sizes, and it makes a colorful display in any flowerpot. Hen and chicks easily propagate as the larger plant (hen) sends out multiple baby sprouts (chicks). These waxy rosettes form tight clusters and will continue to spread as the babies grow and start reproducing on their own. After a few years, the hen will send out a flowering stalk. Once that stalk dies, trim it off. The mother plant will soon fade, as she has reached the end of her life cycle. Remove the plant to make room for the chicks to grow.

STEP-BY-STEP CARE

SOIL: Use a quick-draining soil mixture or cactus soil mix. Or make your own mixture of one-third potting soil, one-third coarse pea gravel, and one-third perlite. Feel free to place an extra layer of pea gravel or other small pebbles at bottom of the pot. This will help drain water away from the soil.

LIGHT: Full sun is preferable. Hen and chicks can tolerate partial sun, but they may not grow as fast or be as colorful.

WATER: Hen and chicks don't like much water. Let the soil dry out completely between waterings. When watering, avoid getting too much moisture on the leaves.

FERTILIZER: Feed with a balanced houseplant fertilizer once a month during spring and summer. For best results, dilute fertilizer to one-quarter strength.

TIP: You can easily remove any baby plants from the mother and transplant them to new containers. The chicks will easily establish themselves and grow if the soil is not too wet.

JADE
PLANT

• Crassula ovata •

Commonly known as the friendship tree, lucky plant, or money tree, the jade plant is a sturdy treelike succulent. Folklore has it that the plant brings an abundance of wealth and prosperity to its owners, perhaps because of the coin-shaped leaves. Jade plants store water in their flat leaves and will do best if you allow the soil to become almost dry between waterings. Jade plants thrive in room temperatures between 65° and 75°F / 18° and 24°C, and can grow up to 5 feet / 1.5 m indoors.

STEP-BY-STEP CARE

SOIL: Use a quick-draining soil mixture or cactus soil mix. Or make your own mixture of one-third potting soil, one-third coarse sand, and one-third perlite. Add coconut coir or peat moss to help with water absorption and aeration.

LIGHT: Jade plants do best when they get four or more hours of direct sunlight every day. Some varieties might develop a red tinge on their leaf edges if given too much sunlight. If this happens, move your plant to a slightly shadier spot.

WATER: Water your jade plant when the top 2 to 3 inches / 5 to 7.5 cm of soil are dry to the touch. Do not overwater, as this will cause roots to rot. Provide less water during the cooler months of winter as the plant goes dormant.

FERTILIZER: Feed with a balanced houseplant fertilizer every two to three weeks during spring and summer. For best results, dilute fertilizer to half strength.

TIP: Your jade plant will enjoy being outdoors during the summer. Put the plant out for the warmer months and bring it inside before signs of the first frost. If your outdoor sunlight is intense, provide light shade in the afternoon, since jade plants are sensitive to sunburn.

• Jasminum polyanthum •

Jasmine is a wonderfully fragrant plant. Its oils are quite popular and can be found in many perfumes, lotions, and herbal remedies. Its sweet-scented white flowers bloom from spring through summer and become more aromatic in the evenings. Jasmine grows profusely in warmer climates and spreads wildly as a climbing vine or bush. Use a small trellis or garden stake to train your vines as they grow. A heavy pruning at the onset of spring will entice your plant to become fuller during the growing season.

STEP-BY-STEP CARE

SOIL: Use good-quality all-purpose potting mix. The addition of coconut coir to your soil will help increase drainage while retaining moisture.

LIGHT: Jasmine plants prefer full to partial sun. Decrease the amount of sunlight during winter.

WATER: Water thoroughly to keep the soil moist. If the saucer under the pot fills with water, empty it. Water less during the winter.

FERTILIZER: Feed with a fertilizer that is higher in phosphorus, such as 5-10-5, every two to three weeks during spring and summer. For best results, dilute fertilizer to half strength. Phosphorus helps lengthen flowers' bloom time.

TIP: Jasmine plants benefit from being exposed to cooler temperatures in the fall. This cold spell will encourage another blooming cycle in the winter. You can even set them outside for about six weeks and then bring them back inside and place them in a south-facing window.

LEMON BUTTON ❊•FERN•❊

• *Nephrolepis cordifolia 'Duffii'* •

The lemon button fern, also known as southern sword fern or erect sword fern, is a small compact yellow-green fern that grows to about 12 inches / 30.5 cm high and wide. Its arching stems have round, button-like leaves that emit a lemony scent when handled. This fern requires little care once it's established and is perfect for growing in a terrarium (see below). The lemon button fern enjoys humid environments and can tolerate temperatures up to 75°F / 24°C.

STEP-BY-STEP CARE

SOIL: Use a well-draining potting soil. Mix peat moss into your soil to help increase the acidic content and retain needed nutrients.

LIGHT: Lemon button ferns require partial shade. Keep them away from direct sun in the afternoon. Decrease the amount of sunlight during winter.

WATER: Water thoroughly to keep the soil moist but not soggy. Do not let the soil dry out between waterings.

FERTILIZER: Feed with a balanced houseplant fertilizer, diluted to half strength, every other week during spring and summer. Do not fertilize in fall and winter.

TIP: If creating a terrarium, first add a 1-inch / 2.5-cm layer of pebbles for proper drainage. Next, add a thin layer of activated charcoal (found at your local garden center), and then a dampened layer of sphagnum moss on top of the charcoal. Mix two parts potting mix with one part sand and add at least 2 to 3 inches / 5 to 7.5 cm to the terrarium. Mist the soil. Place the fern on top of the soil and gently tamp roots down with your fingers or a skewer. Mist the soil again. Do not fertilize unless the plant looks malnourished. If so, feed every five to six weeks with a balanced houseplant fertilizer, diluted to one-quarter strength.

Lily
OF THE
Valley

• Convallaria majalis •

Lily of the valley is often grown indoors during winter to add a touch of spring woodland to the home. This broad-leafed plant sends up shoots of cascading white flowers with a sweet scent. You can purchase lilies of the valley as dormant rhizomes (rootstock), known as pips, typically in the fall. Gently separate the pips and soak them in water for several hours. Trim off 1 to 2 inches / 2.5 to 5 cm of the roots, if needed, to accommodate the depth of your pot. Moisten the soil and place a small amount in the bottom of a pot with good drainage holes. Place pips in the pot with buds facing upward, spaced to about 1 to 2 inches / 2.5 to 5 cm apart. Fill in with soil to just barely cover the tops of the pips, then water liberally. Place the pot in partial sun in a room that is 60° to 70°F / 16° to 21°C.

STEP-BY-STEP CARE

SOIL: Use good-quality all-purpose potting mix. The addition of peat moss will help increase drainage while retaining moisture.

LIGHT: Place the lily of the valley in a bright room with indirect sunlight.

WATER: Keep soil evenly moist but not soggy.

FERTILIZER: Feed monthly with a balanced houseplant fertilizer diluted to half strength while the plant is growing.

TIP: For a longer display of blooms, plant several lilies of the valley at three-week intervals. After the plants have flowered, keep watering and then transplant them to a shady spot in the garden after the last frost.

• Dracaena sanderiana •

Lucky bamboo, also known as friendship bamboo or ribbon plant, is said to bring good fortune and happiness to its owners. Lucky bamboo can be grown in water or soil. If using water, make sure the level is high enough to cover the roots once they emerge. You will need to change the water every couple of weeks and keep your container clean. Use distilled water if chemicals in tap water are a concern. A tall container will help support the lucky bamboo's stalks.

STEP-BY-STEP CARE

SOIL: Use well-draining all-purpose potting mix. Place pebbles underneath your soil to help add drainage.

LIGHT: Place lucky bamboo in a bright room with indirect sunlight. Direct sunlight can cause the leaves to burn.

WATER: If you choose to grow this plant in water, keep the level between 1 and 3 inches / 2.5 and 7.5 cm. If planting in soil, water regularly. Keep soil moist but not soggy.

FERTILIZER: Fertilize every other month with a balanced houseplant fertilizer.

TIP: If growing lucky bamboo in water, use pebbles, glass marbles, or glass gemstones in the bottom of the container to help stabilize the lucky bamboo.

MAIDENHAIR FERN

• Adiantum raddianum •

The maidenhair fern is a soft, lacy evergreen fern that displays well in a flowerpot or hanging basket. This plant enjoys a humid environment sheltered from direct sunlight, much like a damp forest floor. These ferns will grow to about 12 to 24 inches / 30.5 to 61 cm in height and prefer temperatures above 70°F / 21°C. Maidenhair ferns also grow well in open or closed terrariums.

STEP-BY-STEP CARE

SOIL: Use good-quality all-purpose potting mix.

LIGHT: Place the maidenhair fern in partial shade. Direct sunlight can burn the fronds.

WATER: Keep the soil moist but not soggy. If the air is too dry, mist regularly or use a pebble tray to add humidity (see below).

FERTILIZER: Feed monthly during spring and summer with a balanced houseplant fertilizer diluted to half strength.

TIP: A pebble tray adds humidity to the air around your plant. To make your own, fill a waterproof saucer or shallow tray with pebbles, then add water until the level is just below the tops of the pebbles. Place the potted plant on top of the pebbles. Add water when necessary to keep the water level consistent.

• Gymnocalycium mihanovichii •

The moon cactus, or Hibotan cactus, sports a colorful ball-like crown atop its sturdy green base. Brilliant shades of red, pink, orange, and yellow fill the ball, which lacks the chlorophyll that makes the rest of the plant green. The moon cactus is actually a combination of two cacti that have been grafted together. As a seedling, the colorful cactus can't survive on its own without the necessary sugars from photosynthesis, so in order to survive, the seedling must be grafted onto a green rootstock base.

STEP-BY-STEP CARE

SOIL: Use a quick-draining soil mixture or cactus soil mix. Or make your own mixture of one-third potting soil, one-third coarse sand, and one-third perlite.

LIGHT: The moon cactus requires bright indirect sunlight.

WATER: Water the moon cactus thoroughly and let it dry out between waterings. Water less during winter.

FERTILIZER: Feed monthly with a cactus fertilizer during spring and summer.

TIP: The moon cactus looks great planted alone or grouped together in a rainbow of colors.

• Narcissus papyraceus •

Paperwhites are classic flowering bulbs that spring life into your home during the coolness of winter. Delicate white flowers sit atop long slender stems and look beautiful when gently tied together with ribbon or string. Paperwhites come in a variety of hybrids and can be forced to bloom indoors (see below).

STEP-BY-STEP CARE

GROW IN SOIL: Choose a well-draining container 3 to 4 inches / 7.5 to 10 cm tall. Fill with all-purpose potting mix and place the bulbs, tips pointing up, 1 to 2 Inches / 2.5 to 5 cm apart. Gently push the bulbs into the soil so they rest just below the pot's rim. Lightly cover them with soil. Place the pot in a cool location (50° to 60°F / 10° to 16°C) for about two weeks and then move it to a warm, sunny area. Keep the soil moist but not soggy.

GROW IN PEBBLES: Select a glass container or waterproof shallow pot at least 3 inches / 7.5 cm tall. Fill the container halfway with pebbles or marbles and set the bulbs on top, almost touching, with tips pointing up.

Gently add more pebbles or marbles to secure the bulbs. Add water until it reaches the base of the bulbs. Place the pot in a cool location (50 to 60°F / 10 to 16°C) for about two weeks and then move it to a warm, sunny area. Keep the water at the same level.

GROW IN WATER: Place a single bulb in a narrow glass vase or on top of a bottle with a small opening. Add water until it reaches just below the base of the bulb. Place the container in a cool location (50° to 60°F / 10° to 16°C) for about two weeks and then move it to a warm, sunny area. Keep the water at the same level.

> **TIP:** Stake paperwhites with a decorative branch or bamboo if foliage becomes too top-heavy.

• Beaucarnea recurvata •

A drought-tolerant plant, the ponytail palm gets its name from its long, silky leaves that curve downward like wispy tresses of hair. The slow-growing plant has a bulbous trunk that stores water, so drier soils are preferred. Ponytail palms do quite well in a container that is only a few inches wider than its trunk. If there is excess room in the pot, the palm will grow wider and taller as it fills the space. Keeping a smaller container will regulate the overall size of your plant. The ponytail palm enjoys temperatures between 65° and 75°F / 18° to 24°C in the spring, summer, and fall and cooler in the winter.

STEP-BY-STEP CARE

SOIL: Use a quick-draining soil mixture or cactus soil mix. Or make your own mixture of one-third potting soil, one-third coarse sand, and one-third perlite. Add vermicompost to provide extra nutrients and beneficial enzymes.

LIGHT: The ponytail palm enjoys bright indirect or full sun.

WATER: Water the ponytail palm thoroughly and let it dry out significantly between waterings. Ponytail palms prefer drier soil. Water less during winter.

FERTILIZER: Feed monthly with a balanced houseplant fertilizer during spring and summer. Dilute fertilizer to half strength.

TIP: Remove dust from leaves by gently spraying them with room-temperature water and then wiping them clean with a soft cloth or paper towel.

PRICKLY PEAR

• *Opuntia ficus-indica* •

The prickly pear, also known as Indian fig or cactus pear fruit, is a common plant found in Mediterranean and tropical climates. Well-known for its juicy fruit, the prickly pear has teardrop-shaped pads usually covered in sharp white spines. Some species are spineless, while others have small, fuzzy patches of hairlike spines. The prickly pear will boast colorful flowers in shades of white, yellow, or orange, depending on the variety. Keep the cactus healthy by removing damaged pads or those that are overlapping. The prickly pear prefers temperatures ranging from 65° to 90°F / 18° to 32°C in summer and cooler in winter.

STEP-BY-STEP CARE

SOIL: Use a quick-draining soil mixture or cactus soil mix. Or make your own mixture of one-third potting soil, one-third coarse sand, and one-third peat moss.

LIGHT: Place the prickly pear in a window that receives full sun all day.

WATER: Water the prickly pear when the top 1 inch / 2.5 cm of soil is dry to the touch. The prickly pear prefers drier soil. Water less during winter.

FERTILIZER: Feed monthly during spring and summer with a 5-10-10 fertilizer to promote flowering and fruiting.

TIP: Transplant in spring if the prickly pear has become root-bound. Use heavy work gloves and kitchen tongs to handle the spiky pads. Prune any long, heavy limbs or dense areas that have overlapping pads.

• Aechmea fasciata •

A member of the bromeliad family, the silver vase plant, or urn plant, displays a large pink flower after it reaches maturity in a couple of years. Most garden centers will sell this plant already in bloom. Its large, leathery leaves are dappled in a silvery gray and form a vaselike cup in the middle of the plant. You will need to keep this cup filled with water, otherwise the leaves may dry up and turn brown. The silver vase plant prefers temperatures between 65° and 75°F / 18° and 24°C.

STEP-BY-STEP CARE

SOIL: Use good-quality all-purpose potting mix. The addition of peat moss will help with drainage and provide a more acidic environment, which bromeliads prefer.

LIGHT: Place your silver vase plant in a bright location with some direct light. If leaves start turning brown, move the plant out of the direct sun.

WATER: Water the soil around the plant thoroughly and let it dry out between waterings. Keep the inner "vase" of this plant filled with water. If the air is very dry, mist the leaves regularly.

FERTILIZER: Feed monthly with a balanced houseplant fertilizer during spring and summer. Dilute fertilizer to half strength.

TIP: A silver vase plant's flower will last about six months. Once the bloom fades, the plant will send out a few pups (baby plants that emerge near the plant's base). Remove the pups when they are about 6 inches / 15 cm tall and repot them in their own containers. This completes the lifecycle of the main plant, which will eventually lose vitality and die.

SNAKE PLANT

• Sansevieria trifasciata •

The snake plant has stiff pointed leaves that are commonly banded with gold, silver, or gray edges. Commonly referred to as mother-in-law's tongue, the snake plant's upright leaves can grow to between 3 and 4 feet / 91 and 122 cm tall. The snake plant is one of the easiest plants to grow indoors, as it adapts to a variety of growing conditions. An added bonus is that it improves indoor air quality by absorbing toxins, such as nitrogen oxide and formaldehyde.

STEP-BY-STEP CARE

SOIL: Snake plants prefer a loose all-purpose potting mix. Try adding coarse sand to your soil to help with drainage.

LIGHT: Place your snake plant in a bright location with indirect light.

WATER: Water the snake plant thoroughly and let the soil dry out between waterings. Snake plants prefer drier soil. Water less during winter.

FERTILIZER: Feed monthly during spring and summer with a cactus fertilizer.

TIP: Use a clay or terra-cotta pot for your snake plant. These porous containers help draw water out of the soil and away from the roots. Snake plants don't like to sit in soggy soil.

STRING OF PEARLS

• Senecio rowleyanus •

The string of pearls plant, also known as string of beads, is an eye-catching addition to any home. The tendril-like fronds display spherical leaves that resemble a long beaded necklace. The plant looks stunning in a hanging pot either by itself or with other succulents. When potting, press the soil down firmly around the plant to secure it in place. Keep your succulent high enough away from curious pets, as the leaves are toxic if ingested.

STEP-BY-STEP CARE

SOIL: Use a quick-draining soil mixture or cactus soil mix. Or make your own mixture of one-third potting soil, one-third coarse sand, and one-third perlite. Add vermicompost to provide extra nutrients and beneficial enzymes.

LIGHT: Place the string of pearls in a bright, sunny location, preferably a west- or south-facing window. Avoid any cool drafts, as this may cause leaf drop.

WATER: Water every two to three weeks. Remove excess water from the saucer to prevent the soil from becoming soggy. If your container is plastic or some other nonporous material, water less often, as these containers keep soil moist longer. The string of pearls plant prefers drier soil. In winter, water every four to five weeks.

FERTILIZER: Feed every two to three weeks during spring and summer with a balanced houseplant fertilizer diluted to half strength.

TIP: In spring, trim back long and straggly stems to maintain the plant's size and appearance. Healthy cuttings (about 4 inches / 10 cm long) can be repotted into the same container or new soil-filled pots. Roots will quickly grow into new plants.

TULIP

• Tulipa Darwin Hybrid 'Red Impression' •

Purchase bulbs in the fall and chill them for about twelve to fifteen weeks in your garage or refrigerator in temperatures of 35° to 45°F / 2° to 7°C. Keep bulbs in a paper bag and away from fruits and vegetables that emit ethylene, a gas that prevents flowering. After chilling, fill a well-draining container with premoistened potting mix to about 3 inches / 7.5 cm below the rim. With pointy sides up, place the bulbs on the potting mix and cover them with more soil until the tips are barely showing. Gently water and place the pot in a cool, dark location (35° to 50°F / 2° to 10°C), watering once a week. When you see growth, set your bulbs in a slightly warmer location (50° to 65°F / 10° to 18°C) that receives bright indirect light. Your flowers will start to bloom in about two to three weeks.

STEP-BY-STEP CARE

SOIL: Use good-quality all-purpose potting mix.

LIGHT: After growth appears, place the bulbs in a bright location with indirect sun.

WATER: While the bulbs are in a dark location, keep the soil moist but not soggy. Once leaves emerge and you place the plant in a bright location, let the soil dry to the touch between waterings.

FERTILIZER: Feed every two weeks with a balanced houseplant fertilizer diluted to half strength.

TIP: You can force your tulip bulbs to grow in water. Sprinkle a few handfuls of glass beads or pebbles in the bottom of a tall glass vase, then place the chilled bulbs, pointy sides up, on top. Add water until it reaches just below the base of the bulbs. Do not let the water touch the bulbs.

ZEBRA CACTUS

• Haworthia attenuata •

The zebra cactus is a striking little plant that begs to be displayed atop a decorative layer of stone or in a unique container. Much like the aloe plant, its long, pointed leaves extend straight out in all directions. The zebra cactus has bumpy white lines on the outer edges of its leaves resembling a zebra pattern. This small plant usually grows no larger than 6 inches / 15 cm tall.

STEP-BY-STEP CARE

SOIL: Use a cactus and succulent potting mix, or create your own quick-draining soil with one-third potting mix, one-third coarse sand, and one-third perlite.

LIGHT: Place the zebra cactus in a bright, sunny location, preferably a west- or south-facing window.

WATER: Water the zebra cactus thoroughly and let it dry out between waterings. The leaves will turn brown and soft if overwatered. Water less in winter.

FERTILIZER: Feed monthly with a balanced houseplant fertilizer during spring and summer. Dilute fertilizer to half strength.

> **TIP:** Display your zebra cactus atop layers of decorative sand and pebbles in a glass vase. To do so, first plant your zebra cactus in a small glass or plastic container. Place this container in a larger glass vase, then layer in different colored sand or stone around the outside of the potted container to achieve the desired look. Water only the inner container with a large dropper or syringe.

Resources

Tools

GARDENER'S SUPPLY COMPANY
www.gardeners.com

Gardener's Supply Company is a great resource for gardening tools, gloves, soils, and fertilizers with a commitment to the environment.

HOMEBASE
www.homebase.co.uk

At Homebase, you can find reasonably priced pruners, cutting tools, and gardening gloves. Stores are located in the UK.

GARDENISTA
www.gardenista.com

The Indoor Garden section of Gardenista's website offers helpful tips and enticing photos of indoor gardening. You won't leave uninspired or uninformed!

WEST COUNTY GARDENER
www.westcountygardener.com

West County Gardener offers durable, nitrile palm gloves that are waterproof and abrasion resistant. Made with recycled yarn, the gloves are available in four different sizes.

Materials

TERRAIN
www.shopterrain.com

Offering a delightful assortment of spring flowering bulbs, Terrain also carries an eclectic range of terra-cotta and clay pots.

WEST ELM
www.westelm.com

West Elm features a modern collection of vases, containers, and terrariums. You can also find decorative objects to hold air plants.

Plants

AIR PLANT SUPPLY COMPANY
www.airplantsupplyco.com

Here you can find a wide range of air plants, terrariums, containers, and cork bark displays. You can also purchase air plants in a variety of sizes.

CACTUS STORE
www.cactusstore.com

The Cactus Store offers a unique selection of prickly pear cacti and aloe plants, along with other interesting cactus species.

HIRT'S GARDENS
www.hirts.com

Hirt's Gardens provides a wonderful selection of houseplants, terrarium plants, cacti, and succulents. Many plants can be purchased already potted in decorative containers.

CROCUS
www.crocus.co.uk

Crocus offers close to one hundred types of houseplants, complete with homecare instructions.

MOSS ACRES
www.mossacres.com

Moss Acres features a variety of mosses and kits to create your own terrarium, and also provides a lot of useful information on growing moss.

Acknowledgments

CREATING THIS BOOK was a dream come true—combining my two loves of art and gardening.

A special thanks to Bridget Watson Payne for giving me the opportunity and seeing my art as an illustrated book, and to Laura Lee Mattingly, who provided the needed wisdom, structure, and patience to shape this book into a reality. Amy Treadwell and Jean Blomquist, your attention to detail and accuracy offers greater gardening success. Allison Weiner, thank you for your amazing design aesthetic!

A big thank you to Mom and Dad, who tirelessly followed me along my creative journey, and to Clark and Karen, for giving me the support I very much needed. And most of all, an enormous thank you to my husband, Bret, for his generous heart and endless patience. My children, Cole, Mia, and Ella, you make me smile more than words or pictures can ever tell.